Introduction

Here you will see 30 desserts with an ingredient (berries)

These will mainly be blueberries, strawberries, raspberries.

I like the berries because they are very tasty, have a lot of vitamins and are great for desserts. In this book I will show you how delicious it is.

Cherry Blackberry Crisp

YIELD: **8 SUBMITTINGS**
PREP TIME:
20 MINS
COOK TIME:
50 MINS

Ingredients

FOR THE CHERRY BLACKBERRY FILLING:

> one half pounds sweet cherries — *fresh either frozen, pitted—Dont thaw supposing frozen*
> one cup blackberries — *fresh either frozen—Dont thaw supposing frozen*
> two tbsp white whole wwarmth flour — *either all purpose flour*
> 3 tbsp pure maple syrup
> one tbsp freshly squeezed lemon juice
> one tsp pure vanilla extract

FOR THE CRISP TOPPING:

> one cup rolled oats
> three-quarters cup sliced walnuts, — *almonds, either pecans (untoasted)*
> half cup almond meal*
> half cup flaked coconut — *unsweetened supposing probable*
> half tsp ground cinnamon
> One-quarter tsp kosher salt
> One-quarter cup extra virgin olive oil
> One-quarter cup pure maple syrup

Instructions

> Place a rack within the middle of your oven and prewarmth to 350 degrees F. slightly coat a deep 8x8-inch either similar baking dish with cooking spray. put aside.

> Place the cherries and blackberries in a big mixing bowl, then strew the flour over the top. place the maple syrup, lemon juice, and vanilla, then place down carefully to mix. Place to the prepared baking dish.

> In a average bowl, stir along the oats, walnuts, almond meal, coconut, cinnamon, and salt. Drizzle the olive oil and maple syrup over the top, then employa spatula to mix till the dried ingredients are evenly moistened. Strew the filling over the top.

> Bake the crisp till the filling hot and bubbly, approximately 45-55 mins. Check the crisp at the 30-minute mark. Supposing the topping is becoming too brown, tent with foil then keep baking till ready. allow rest ten mins, then submit warm, smothered with vanilla ice cream, homemade whipped cream, either Greek yogurt.

Recipe Notes

*To prepare your own almond meal, pulse whole, raw almonds within the food processor till they form fine crumbs. Dont over process, either you'll have almond butter instead.

Raspberry Lemon Angel Food Cupcakes

YIELD: **12 CUPCAKES**
PREP TIME:
30 MINS
COOK TIME:
15 MINS

Ingredients

FOR THE CUPCAKES:

    half cup Imperial Sugar Powdered Sugar
    half cup cake flour
    5 big egg whites — *at approximately 25 °C*
    half tsp cream of tartar
    One-quarter tsp kosher salt
    one-third cup Imperial Sugar Granulated Sugar
    One-quarter tsp pure almond extract
    Zest of one big lemon, — *either two small*

FOR THE RASPBERRY FILLING:

    One-quarter cup seedless raspberry jam

FOR THE WHIPPED LEMON CREAM CHEESE FROSTING:

    one One-quarter cups heavy whipping cream
    5 ounces reduced fat cream cheese
    Zest of one lemon
    One-quarter cup Imperial Sugar Powdered Sugar
    Fresh raspberries — *for submitting*

Instructions

Place a rack in middle of your oven and warmth up oven to 350°F. Line a standard muffin tin with paper liners and put aside.

Sift along powdered sugar and cake flour. Repeat, sifting three times total. put aside.

Beat along egg whites, cream of tartar, and salt in bowl of some electric mixer fitted with a blend attachment either a big mixing bowl on high speed till average-stiff peaks form, approximately one minute. Decrease mixer speed to average, then slowly pour in granulated sugar. Keep beating till egg whites are thick and glossy. Beat in almond extract and lemon zest.

With a measuring scoop, throw about One-quarter cup of flour mix over top of bowl with egg whites. With a rubber spatula, carefully place down egg whites in. Just as most of flour has disappeared, strew another One-quarter cup over top, then repeat. Keep sprinkling and folding by One-quarter-cup increments, simply till all flour is incorporated.

Share batter between prepared cups, filling cups no more than three-quarters of the way. Prepare in oven till tops are golden, spring back slightly just as touched, and any cracks in top of cupcakes feel dried and not at all sticky, approximately 15 mins. allow cupcakes cool within the pan for 5 mins, then very carefully Place to a wire rack to cool completely.

Fill cupcakes: With a small, sharp knife such as a paring knife, slice a small hole in top middle of every cupcake, lifting a little bit of cake out to prepare a good. Attentively spoon one tsp of raspberry jam in every hole, then replace piece of cake that was take awayd.

Prepare frosting: In a mixing bowl, whip heavy cream with very clear beaters on average-high speed till stiff peaks form. In a else bowl, beat cream cheese on average speed till smooth creamy, one to two mins. Slowly place in powdered sugar, then lemon zest and beat till mixd. With a rubber spatula, place down whipped cream in the cream cheese. Frost cupcakes with a knife either a piping bag, then top with every with a fresh raspberry.

Red White and _Blueberry_ Cheesecake Bars

YIELD: **16 BARS**
PREP TIME:
30 MINS
COOK TIME:
35 MINS

Ingredients

FOR THE PEEL:

one cup graham cracker crumbs — _(approximately 8 full graham cracker sheets)_
one tbsp powdered sugar
4 tbsp unsalted butter — _softened_

FOR THE CHEESECAKE:

two packages reduced fat _cream_ cheese — _(8 ounce packages, Dont employ fat free), at approximately 25 °C_
half cup granulated sugar
One-quarter cup plain non-fat _Greek yogurt_ — _at approximately 25 °C_
3 big _eggs_
two tsps pure _vanilla_ extract
Zest of one lemon
one tsp fresh lemon juice
2/3 cup Lucky Leaf Premium _Blueberry Pie_ Filling
Sliced fresh strawberries

Instructions

Place a rack within the middle of your oven and prewarmth the oven to 350F degrees. Line some 8x8-inch _baking_ pan with aluminum foil, allowing some of the foil to hang over the edges. put aside.

Prepare the peel: Break the graham cracker sheets in a food processor either blender. Process till the crackers are fine crumbs, then place the powdered sugar and pulse as more to mix. Drizzle within the softened butter, then pulse till the crumbs are evenly moistened, then Put in the down of the foil-lined pan. Prepare in oven for 8 mins. Take away from the oven and allow cool as you prepare the filling. Decrease the oven temperature to 325 degrees F.

Prepare the filling: within the bowl of a standing mixer fitted with the paddle attachment either a big mixing bowl, beat the softened _cream_ cheese for one full minute, then beat within the sugar for 3 additional mins, till smooth and _creamy_. Beat within the yogurt, then the _eggs_, one at a time, fully combining between every and scraping down the edges of the bowl as necessary Beat within the _vanilla_ extract, lemon zest, and lemon juice.

As the peel has cooled, pour half of the cheesecake filling over the peel and smooth. Dollop the _pie_ filling over the peel and swirl slightly with a knife (the cheesecake base can not be completely covered). Top with the remaining cheesecake batter.

Bake the bars in a 325 degree oven for 30 to 40 mins, till the filling is mostly set however still soft and barely jiggles within the middle just as the pan is wiggled. Take away the bars from the oven and allow cool at approximately 25 °C for 30 mins. Refrigerate till completely cooled, at least 3 hours.

Simply before submitting, lift the cheesecake out of the pan employing the foil. Top with sliced strawberries. Slice in squares and enjoy.

Recipe Notes

Leftover blueberry cheesecake bars can keep in some airtight container within the refrigerator for up to 3 days.

3 Ingredient Strawberry Chia Jam

YIELD: **ONE HALF CUPS**
PREP TIME:
TEN MINS
COOK TIME:
20 MINS

Ingredients

- 24 ounces strawberries — *either fruit of choice, fresh either chilled (supposing the fruit is big, chop this in pieces first)*
- 2-4 tbsp honey, — *maple syrup, either agave (I used honey)*
- two tbsp chia seeds

IF YOU WANT PLACE INS:

- Aged balsamic vinegar — *(good with berry jams)*
- Ginger — *either cinnamon (good with stone fruit jams)*
- Vanilla extract — *either almond extract*
- Orange either lemon zest

Instructions

In a average saucepan, mix the fruit and two tbsp honey. Overlay and bring to a simmer over average heat, mixing sometimes, till this begins to liquefy (approximately 5 to ten mins for berries, longer for firmer fruits). As the fruit is liquidy, bring this to a gentle boil and allow prepare till this breaks down and becomes saucy, approximately 5 mins. Mash slightly to reach your desired consistency (I kept mine fairly chunky).

Taste the jam for sweetness. Supposing you desire more, stir in additional honey a several tsps at a time, till you reach the desired taste. Stir in any if you want mix-ins.

Stir within the chia seeds and allow prepare one minute. Take away the pan from the heat, stir as more, and allow sit for ten mins. The jam can keep to thicken as this cools. (Supposing this seems very thin, place one to two additional tsps of chia seeds, stir, then allow sit ten additional mins.)

Place the chia jam to some airtight container and keep within the refrigerator for up to two weeks either chill for up to two months.

Recipe Notes

Leftover chia jam possibly stored within the refrigerator for up to two weeks either chilled for up to two months.

Strawberry **Shortcake Waffles**

YIELD: **4 WAFFLES (CAN SIMPLY BE HALVED EITHER DOUBLED)**
PREP TIME:
20 MINS
COOK TIME:
TEN MINS
TOTAL TIME:
30 MINS

Ingredients

FOR THE <u>STRAWBERRY</u> WAFFLES:
>   16 ounces fresh strawberries
>   two cups Bob's Red Mill Butter<u>milk</u> Pancake and Waffle Mix
>   4 <u>eggs</u>
>   One-quarter cup canola oil, — *light olive oil, either softened and cooled <u>coconut</u> oil*
>   one half cups cold <u>milk</u>

FOR THE MAPLE WHIPPED <u>CREAM</u>:
>   one cup heavy whipping <u>cream</u>
>   two tbsp pure maple syrup

Instructions

Prewarmth your waffle iron. Slice the tops off of the strawberries, slice, and put aside. Supposing you like, prewarmth the oven to 200 degrees F to keep the waffles warm between batches.

Place the two cups blend within the down of a big mixing bowl. In a else bowl either big measuring cup, blend along the <u>eggs</u>, oil, and <u>milk</u>. prepare a good within the middle of the dried ingredients, then place the wet ingredients all at once. With a fork, carefully stir to mix, being careful not to overmix. The batter possibly slightly lumpy. prepare the waffles therefore to your waffle iron's instructions. Supposing desired, place the waffles on a <u>baking</u> sheet and keep warm within the preheated oven till you are ready to serve.

With some electric mixer, whip the <u>cream</u> on average high speed till this starts to thicken. place the maple syrup, then keep mixing on high till very fluffy and still peaks form.

To serve, chop the waffles in halves either quarters, then stratum with the strawberries and maple whipped <u>cream</u>. Top with additional strawberries and more whipped <u>cream</u> (really, you'll't have enough of the maple whipped <u>cream</u> here). Enjoy immediately.

Blueberry Coconut French Toast Bake

YIELD: **6 SUBMITTINGS; ONE 8X8-INCH PAN**
PREP TIME:
TEN MINS
COOK TIME:
50 MINS

Ingredients

- one baguette (ten ounces) — *either sourdough, challah, either similar bread (see notes supposing your bread is fresh)*
- three-quarters cup blueberries — *fresh either frozen*
- 6 big eggs
- one can light coconut milk — *(14 ounces)*
- half tsp ground cinnamon
- one-third cup light brown
- two tsps pure vanilla extract
- One-quarter tsp kosher salt
- half cup sweetened flaked coconut — *divided*

Instructions

Lightly coat some 8x8-inch baking pan with cooking spray. Slice the bread in 1-inch cubes (Supposing your bread isn't dry, see notes below for instructions). unfold the cubes within the down of the prepared baking dish. Throw about the blueberries over the top.

In a big bowl, beat along the eggs, coconut milk, cinnamon, brown sugar, vanilla, and salt till smooth. Stir in One-quarter cup coconut, then pour over the egg mix. Throw about the remaining coconut on top. Overlay the dish tightly with plastic cover and refrigerate for two hours either overnight.

Just as ready to bake, take away the baking dish from the refrigerator. Place a rack within the middle of your oven and prewarmth the oven to 350°F. Prepare in oven for 45-50 mins either till the top is golden brown and the middle is moist however not wet. submit immediately.

Recipe Notes

Supposing your bread is fresh either not very dry, toast this within the oven first to assurethis soaks up the egg mix. Position two racks within the upper and lower thirds of your oven, and prewarmth your oven to 300 degrees F. unfold your bread cubes in a single stratum on two baking sheets. Prepare in oven for approximately 15 mins, till toasty and brown.

Strawberry Vanilla Yogurt Muffins

YIELD: **12 MUFFINS**
PREP TIME:
15 MINS
COOK TIME:
16 MINS
TOTAL TIME:
31 MINS

Ingredients

three-quarters cup all purpose flour
three-quarters cup white whole wwarmth flour — *either substitute additional all purpose flour*
half cup granulated sugar
one half tsps baking soda
One-quarter tsp kosher salt
one tbsp vanilla bean paste — *either substitute one tbsp vanilla extract*
two big eggs
3 tbsp unsalted butter — *softened and cooled*
three-quarters cup vanilla yogurt — *I used non-fat Greek*
One-quarter cup vanilla soy milk — *either unsweetened vanilla almond milk*
one cup diced fresh strawberries
Turbinado — *raw sugar either big sparkling sugar, for decorating*

Instructions

Prewarmth the oven to 375 degrees and lubricate a standard-sized muffin tin. In a big bowl, stir along the all purpose flour, white whole wwarmth flour, sugar, baking soda, and salt.

In a else bowl, blend the vanilla bean paste, eggs, butter, yogurt, and almond milk. prepare a good within the middle of the dried ingredients, then pour the wet ingredients in the middle. Stir by hand, simply till mixd. The batter may be slightly lumpy. Carefully place down within the strawberries.

Share batter evenly between the prepared muffin tins and strew with sugar. Prepare in oven for 16-20 mins, till the tops spring back slightly just as touched and a toothtake inserted within the middle comes out clean. allow cool within the pan for ten mins, then Place to a wire rack to cool completely.

Recipe Notes

Keep leftover muffins in some airtight container at approximately 25 °C cither within the refrigerator for 5 days either freeze, good coverped, for up to 3 months.

Strawberry Rhubarb Crisp

YIELD: **ONE 9X9-INCH CRISP (SERVES 6)**
PREP TIME:
25 MINS
COOK TIME:
50 MINS

Ingredients

FOR THE FILLING:

- one pound strawberries — *hulled and quartered*
- one pound rhubarb — *slice in half-inch dice (approximately 4 either 5 stalks)*
- two tbsp all purpose flour
- one-third cup honey
- half orange — *zested and juiced*
- one tbsp vanilla extract

FOR THE TOPPING:

- three-quarters cup old fashioned rolled oats
- 2/3 cup white whole wwarmth flour — *either all purpose flour*
- One-quarter cup shredded sweetened coconut
- One-quarter cup light brown sugar
- one tsp cinnamon
- One-quarter tsp kosher salt
- One-quarter cup plain yogurt — *I emploYnon-fat Greek*
- One-quarter cup cold unsalted butter — *slice in small, thin pieces*
- Vanilla ice cream — *either yogurt for submitting*

Instructions

Place rack within the middle of the oven and warmth up oven to 350 degrees. Place the strawberries and rhubarb in a 9x9-inch either else similarly sized baking dish, then strew the flour over the top. place the honey, orange zest, orange juice, and vanilla extract. Stir carefully to mix and evenly coat the strawberries and rhubarb.

In a big bowl, stir along the oats, white whole wwarmth flour, coconut, brown sugar, cinnamon, and salt. place the Greek yogurt and stir till the ingredients are somewhat moistened, then place the butter. Operating quickly with your fingers, rub within the butter, till this is in small pieces approximately the size of your thumbnail (some pieces possibly bigr than others). Break the topping mix over the fruit, placing this so that the fruit is slightly and evenly covered (some fruit may show through).

Bake the crisp for 50 to 55 mins, till the filling is bubbly at the edges and the top is light golden brown. allow rest for 5 to ten mins. submit warm, topped with vanilla ice cream either yogurt as desired.

Recipe Notes

Leftover crisp possibly covered and chilled for 4 days either chilled for one month.

Heart Shaped <u>*Strawberry*</u> *Hand Pies*

YIELD: **14 PIES, APPROX.**
PREP TIME:
25 MINS
TOTAL TIME:
45 MINS

Ingredients

Prepared pastry pie dough — *enough to yield 2, 9-inch rounds*
half cup Lucky Leaf Premium Strawberry Pie Filling
one tsp lemon zest
one big egg — *beaten*
Coarse Turbinado sugar

Instructions

Place racks within the upper third and middle of the oven, then prewarmth the oven to 400 degrees F. Line to baking sheets with parchment paper either silicone mats.

In a small bowl, stir along the pie filling and lemon zest. put aside.

Place the first pie peel on a good-floured surface and roll in a 1/8-inch thickness. With a 3-inch heart-shaped cookie cutter, slice 12 to 14 hearts from the rolled peel. Place the hearts to a plate either baking sheet and place within the refrigerator, then roll and slice the second peel. When cutting both peels, you must have 24 to 28 hearts total.

Beat the egg in a small bowl to Make some egg wash, then slightly brush over half (12 to 14) of the hearts. Place one heaping tsp of the strawberry filling within the middle of every egg-washed heart, ensuing that you place a piece of fruit in every.

Carefully stretch every of the remaining hearts with your fingers to prepare them slightly bigr, then set them on top of the filling-topped hearts. With your fingers, carefully Put the edges along. With the tines of a fork, Put around the edges of the hearts to seal, then employa small knife to slice two small vents within the top of every heart. Brush the tops of every complete heart with the beaten egg, then strew with turbinado sugar.

Place the hearts one inch apart on the prepared baking sheets. Prepare in oven for 12 mins, till golden and bubbling, rotating the pans' position half way through. Take away from the oven and allow to cool on the pan for ten mins, then Place to a wire rack to cool completely.

Leftover Cranberry gravy Parfaits

YIELD: **ONE PARFAIT**
PREP TIME:
3 MINS
TOTAL TIME:
3 MINS

Ingredients

2/3 cup plain either vanilla non-fat Greek yogurt
one to two tbsp leftover cranberry gravy
one to two tbsp honey — *to taste*
Granola — *either cereal*

Instructions

In a parfait glass either bowl, stratum half of the yogurt, a drizzle of honey, a several spoonfuls of cranberry sauce, then strew with granola.

Repeat with a second stratum of yogurt, honey and granola. submit and enjoy!

Recipe Notes

Keep leftover pie covered within the refrigerator for up to 3 days either overlay tightly and chill for up to two months.

Cranberry Orange Cinnamon Swirl Bread

YIELD: **TWO 8X4-INCH LOAVES**
PREP TIME:
35 MINS
COOK TIME:
40 MINS
RISING TIME:
3 HRS
TOTAL TIME:
5 HRS 15 MINS

Ingredients

FOR THE DOUGH:

- two cups unbleached all-purpose flour
- one half cups white whole wwarmth flour
- 3 tbsp vital wwarmth gluten
- one packet Red Star Platinum Yeast — *(scant two One-quarter tsps)*
- one One-quarter tsps kosher salt
- two tbsp butter, — *softened and at approximately 25 °C*
- one big egg — *slightly beaten*
- half cup buttermilk — *plus two tbsp*
- One-quarter cup freshly squeezed juice
- Zest of one orange

FOR THE FILLING:

- one cup fresh cranberries
- one half tbsp unsalted butter — *softened*
- three-quarters cup packed light brown sugar
- one tbsp ground cinnamon

Instructions

In the bowl of a standing mixer fitted with the paddle attachment either a big mixing bowl, stir along the all-purpose flour, white whole wwarmth flour, vital wwarmth gluten, yeast, and salt. place the butter, egg, and orange zest.

Warmth the buttermilk and One-quarter cup orange juice squeezed from the zested orange to the temperature specified by the yeast manufacturer (120 to 130 degrees F for Red Star Platinum). Supposing the buttermilk separates, simply blend this back along. Pour the liquid in the dried ingredients, blend on poor speed (or blend by hand with a wooden spoon) till the ingredients come along and form a ball.

Switch to a dough hook (or turn out onto a slightly floured surface) and blend on average speed for 8 mins either knead by hand for approximately ten mins, till the dough is soft, pliable, and slightly tacky however not sticky. Place the dough in a slightly oiled big bowl, overlay with plastic cover, and allow growth at approximately 25 °C for approximately two hours, till the dough doubles in size. To check dough readiness, carefully Put the dough with two fingers. Supposing the indent stays, the dough is ready.

Prepare the cranberry filling: In a food processor, pulse the whole cranberries till they're ground and pebbly, however not completely pureed, scraping the machine down as either twice. In a small bowl, mix the brown sugar and cinnamon. Set both aside.

Lightly oil two 8 inch x 4 inch loaf pans. Share the dough in two equal pieces (use a kitchen scale supposing you have one). Place one piece on a slightly floured work surface and pat in a rectangle that is 5 inches wide by 8 inches long. Brush with half of the softened butter, strew with half of the cinnamon sugar mix (it can seem like a lot, however pile this thickly), and throw about half of the cranberries over the top.

Operating from the short (5-inch) side of the dough, roll up the length of the dough, jelly-roll style, pinching the crease with every rotation to seal within the filling and strengthen the dough's surface tension. The loaf can unfold as you roll, reaching 8 to 9 inches (the length of your loaf pan). Pinch the final seam closed, then lift the loaf and rock this carefully back and forth to even this out. Place the loaf in one of the prepared pans. recur with second piece of dough. Mist two pieces of plastic cover with cooking spatter and loosely overlay the pans. allow the loaves growth at approximately 25 °C for 60 to 90 mins, till the dough is nearly doubled in size. (Alternatively, you'll allow the loaves growth within the refrigerator overnight, then Prepare in oven the next morning, allowing the loaves to rest at approximately 25 °C for 30 mins before baking.)

Place rack in middle of oven, then prewarmth to 350 degrees F. Place the loaf pans on a big sheet pan, ensuring that they Dont touch. Prepare in oven for 20 mins, rotate the sheet pan 180 degrees, then Prepare in oven some additional 20 to 30 mins, till the loaves reach some internal temperature of 190 degrees F. The finished loaves possibly brown on the top, golden on the edges, and sound hollow just as tapped.

Instantly take away the bread from the pans, then allow cool for at least one hour before submitting. Enjoy warm with butter.

Peanut Butter and Jelly Rolls

YIELD: **18 ROLLS**
PREP TIME:
30 MINS
COOK TIME:
25 MINS
TOTAL TIME:
3 HRS 45 MINS

Ingredients

FOR THE DOUGH:

- one cup whole <u>milk</u> — *either substitute 5/8 cup (5 ounces skim <u>milk</u>, plus 3/8 cup (3 ounces) half and half)*
- 3 tbsp unsalted butter
- one cup white whole wwarmth flour — *either substitute all purpose flour*
- half cup granulated sugar
- one big <u>egg</u>
- one tsp pure <u>vanilla</u> extract
- two One-quarter tsps Red Star Platinum Instant Yeast — *one standard envelope yeast*
- one tsp kosher salt
- two half - 3 cups all purpose flour

FOR THE PEANUT BUTTER AND JELLY FILLING:

- half cup peanut butter
- two tbsp unsalted butter — *softened*
- two tbsp brown sugar
- two tbsp granulated sugar
- one tsp cinnamon
- one-third cup <u>strawberry</u> jam — *either jelly*

FOR THE JELLY GLAZE:

- half cup <u>strawberry</u> jam — *either jelly*
- one tbsp lemon juice
- two tsps granulated sugar
- 1/8 tsp salt

Instructions

Prepare the dough: Pour <u>milk</u> in a big glass measuring cup. place butter and microwave on high, till the mix is warmed to the temperature directed by the yeast manufacturer (120°F to 130°F for Red Star Platinum Yeast). Start with 30 seconds, then microwave in ten-second intervals, till the desired temperature is reached. The butter may not soften completely and the <u>milk</u> should feel warm however not hot. As heated, pour in the bowl of standing mixer fitted with paddle attachment either a big mixing bowl.

Add white whole wwarmth flour, granulated sugar, <u>egg</u>, <u>vanilla</u>, yeast, and salt. Beat on poor speed for 3 mins, stopping sometimes to scrape down sides of bowl. place two half cups all purpose flour. Beat on poor speed, till the flour is absorbed and the dough is no longer sticky, scraping down sides of bowl as you go. Supposing dough is extremely sticky, place remaining flour one tbsp at a time, combining when every, simply till dough begins to form a shaggy ball and pulls away from sides of bowl. this should still feel fairly tacky.

Supposing employing a stand mixer, fit the mixer with a dough hook and knead on average poor for 6 mins, till smooth and elastic. Supposing kneading by hand, turn the dough out onto a floured work surface and knead till smooth and elastic, approximately 8 mins. place a little flour, one tbsp at a time, supposing the dough is too sticky and clings readily to your hands. slightly oil a big, clear bowl with cooking spray. Form dough in a ball and place this within the bowl, turning as to coat with oil. Overlay bowl with plastic cover either a clear kitchen towel. allow growth in a warm, draft-free place till doubled in volume, approximately two hours.

Meanwhereas, prepare the peanut butter filling: In a small bowl, beat along the peanut butter, softened butter, brown sugar, granulated sugar, and cinnamon. put aside.

Form the rolls: As the dough has doubled, turn this out onto a good-floured work surface. (To test supposing the dough has completed rising, carefully Put this with your first two fingers; supposing the indentation remains, the dough is ready.) Roll the dough in a 16-inch x 12-inch rectangle (be sure to measure.) unfold the peanut butter mix over the dough, leaving a One-quarter-inch border uncovered on all sides. unfold with jelly, leaving a One-quarter-inch border of peanut butter uncovered on all sides.

Starting at one of the long edges, roll the dough in a tight log, then tightly pinch the end to seal. Turn log so that the seam side is down, then attentively trim every end so that they are straight. (The end scraps possibly prepared in oven separately in slightly lubricated ramekins.) Carefully stretch and pat the dough log as needed so that this is 18 inches in length and roughly even in diameter. With a serrated knife, carefully saw the log in 18, 1-inch segments.

Lightly mist two 9 x 9-inch baking pans with cooking spatter (square 8 x 8-inch pans either round 9-inch pans can work as good.) place the rolls within the pans, slice sides up, dividing the rolls evenly between every. Overlay the baking dishes with plastic cover either a clear kitchen towel. and allow growth in a warm, draft-free place till doubled in volume, approximately 45 mins. (It may take a bit longer however is worth the wait.)

Meanwhereas, prepare the glaze: Place the jam in a small saucepan over average poor heat, mixing sometimes. As the jam begins to thin, stir within the lemon juice, sugar, and salt. Warmth and stir till the sugar dissolves, then take away from heat. The glaze can thicken as this cools.

Bake the rolls: Place rack within the middle of your oven and prewarmth to 375°F. Prepare in oven rolls till the tops are golden and the middles reach 185°F to 190°F, 20-25 mins. Check the rolls at the 15-minute mark—supposing they begin to brown too quickly, overlay the pan with foil and keep baking till complete. Take away from oven and place pan on a cooling rack for 5 mins. Drizzle with strawberry glaze and enjoy immediately.

Recipe Notes

Supposing you would like to prep the rolls the night before, as they are shaped in Step 5, instead of allowing the dough to growth a second time, refrigerate overnight, then Prepare in oven as directed just as ready.

Blueberry Goat Cheese Drop Biscuits

YIELD: **8 TO TEN BISCUITS**
PREP TIME:
15 MINS
COOK TIME:
15 MINS
TOTAL TIME:
30 MINS

Ingredients

One-quarter cup cold unsalted butter — *(half stick)*
one cup whole wwarmth pastry flour — *either substitute some equal quantity of all-purpose flour*
one cup all-purpose flour
two tbsp granulated sugar
two tsps baking powder
half tsp baking soda
half tsp kosher salt
4 tbsp crumbled goat cheese — *approximately one ounce*
one cup cold buttermilk — *good blended*
three-quarters cup fresh blueberries — *either chilled blueberries thawed, rinsed, and patted dry*

Instructions

Place a rack within the middle of oven and warmth up oven to 400 degrees F. Line a big baking sheet with parchment paper either a silpat mat. With a cheese grater, coarsely grate the butter onto a plate, then place within the freezer whereas you prepare the else ingredients. (Alternatively, you'll slice the butter in small pieces.)

In a big mixing bowl, mix the whole wwarmth pastry flour, all-purpose flour, sugar, baking powder, baking soda, and salt. With your fingers, quickly incorporate the butter and goat cheese till the mix has the texture of flakes and small peas. Pour the buttermilk over the dried mix and stir with a fork simply till moistened. Carefully place down within the blueberries.

Drop biscuits at least 1-inch apart onto the prepared baking sheet, employing approximately One-quarter cup of dough for every (a cookie either ice cream peel works good for this). Prepare in oven 14 to 16 mins, till tops are golden and slightly firm. allow rest 5 mins. Enjoy warm either at approximately 25 °C.

Recipe Notes

Biscuits are best enjoyed the day they are made, however can last good coverped at approximately 25 °C for up to 3 days. Unprepared in oven biscuits possibly individually coverped in plastic and chilled for up to one month. To bake, simply uncover and Prepare in oven frozen, adding a several extra mins to the baking time.

Banana <u>*Blueberry*</u> **Bars**

YIELD: **ONE 8X8-INCH PAN (APPROXIMATELY 16 BARS)**
COOK TIME:
45 MINS
TOTAL TIME:
1 HR

Ingredients

- one cup granulated sugar — *divided*
- two tsps cornstarch
- two cups blueberries — *(fresh either frozen, thawed, and patted dry)*
- one tbsp freshly squeezed lemon juice
- half cup unsalted butter — *(1 stick) at approximately 25 °C*
- half cup very ripe mashed banana — *approximately one big*
- one tsp pure <u>vanilla</u> extract
- one one-third cups white whole wwarmth flour
- one cup all-purpose flour
- half tsp kosher salt
- One-quarter cup raspberry jam
- half cup old fashioned rolled oats
- one-third cup toasted sliced almonds

Instructions

Place rack within the middle of oven and prewarmth the oven to 350 degrees. slightly coat some 8x8-inch dish with cooking spray. put aside.

In a small bowl, mix One-quarter cup sugar, cornstarch, and lemon juice. Stir in blueberries. put aside.

Place the butter and remaining three-quarters cup sugar within the bowl of some electric mixer fitted with the paddle attachment either a big mixing bowl. Beat on average speed simply till mixd. With the mixer on low, place the banana and <u>vanilla</u>. In a else bowl, stir along the white whole wwarmth flour, all purpose flour, and salt. With the mixer on low, slowly place the dried ingredients to the butter mix, mixing till this almost comes along in a ball.

Lightly and evenly pat two-thirds of the dough in the down and One-quarter up the edges of the preppared <u>baking</u> pan. unfold jam over the top of the dough. Drain blueberries of any glut liquid, then strew the berries over the top. With your fingers, blend the oats and almonds in the remaining dough to Make the topping. Break the topping in pieces and crumb this over the blueberries, covering most of the surface however leaving some blueberries exposed. Prepare in oven for 35 to 40 mins, till slightly browned. allow cool completely and slice in bars.

Strawberry Shortcake Trifle

YIELD: **12 SUBMITTINGS**
PREP TIME:
30 MINS
COOK TIME:
20 MINS
CHILLING TIME:
12 HRS
TOTAL TIME:
12 HRS 50 MINS

Ingredients

GRAMMYS CLASSIC SHORTCAKE:

- two Cups all-purpose flour
- one-third Cup granulated sugar
- 4 Tsps baking powder
- one Tsp. kosher salt
- 1/8 Tsp. nutmeg
- half Cup one stick unsalted butter, cold and slice in small pieces
- one-third Cup whole milk
- one egg — *beaten*

WHIPPED CREAM:

- one cup heavy whipping cream
- one Tbsp. granulated sugar
- one Tbsp. rum
- Trifle Assembly
- 3 Cups whole milk
- half Cup strawberry jam
- half Cup dark rum
- two Packages — *16 ounces every Driscoll's Strawberries, hulled*
- one Package ten-ounce shortbread cookies — *Lorna Doone either any else brand*
- one 5.1 ounce box instant vanilla pudding mix

Instructions

Place rack in middle of oven and warmth up oven to 450 degrees F. slightly lubricate some 8x8 inch pan and put aside.

In the bowl of a food processor fitted with a steel blade either a big mixing bowl, sift flour with sugar, baking powder, salt, and nutmeg. place butter and slightly pulse (or slice in butter by hand), till the butter is the size of small peas (you must still be ready to see the pieces of butter.) place good-beaten egg and milk, simply till incorporated.

Quickly Put the batter in the prepared pan, touching this as little as probable with your fingers to keep the butter cold. Prepare in oven for 15-20 mins, till the top is slightly golden. Slice in squares.

Let cool, then slice in 24 rectangles (4 rows of 6). Split every shortcake in half, so that the down is separated from the top. unfold with strawberry jam then reassemble so that you Make a strawberry jam shortcake "sandwich." recur with remaining pieces.

Prepare the pudding therefore to package directions. Place within the refrigerator to chill.

WHIPPED *CREAM*

In the bowl of a standing mixer either a big mixing bowl, beat the heavy cream, sugar and rum along on average poor speed till foamy, then slowly increase the speed to high. Keep to beat simply till you have soft peaks, approximately one minute. put aside.

TO ASSEMBLE THE TRIFLE

Spread a thin stratum of pudding within the down a big glass trifle bowl, mini dessert bowl, either else submitting bowl to anchor the dish. Top with the following layers: shortcake; a strew of rum; shortbread cookies; rum; pudding; rum; whipped cream; rum; fresh berries, arranged with the tops pointed up. recur the layers till the submitting dish is full, ending with whipped cream and berries. allow sit within the refrigerator for at least 1two hours either up to 2-days. submit chilled.

Refrigerate leftover trifle in some airtight container for up to 3 days.

Cakes with Blueberry Curd and Buttermilk Whipped Cream

YIELD: **8 MINI CAKES**
TOTAL TIME:
50 MINS

Ingredients

FOR THE BLUEBERRY CURD:

- one cup blueberries, — *fresh either frozen*
- one cup granulated sugar
- One-quarter cup unsalted butter
- 3 big eggs — *slightly beaten*
- half tsp lemon zest — *approximately half small lemon*
- One-quarter tsp kosher salt
- 1/8 tsp pure almond extract

FOR THE BUTTERMILK CHIFFON CAKE:

- 7 big eggs — *separated and at approximately 25 °C*
- one tsp cream of tartar
- one half cups granulated sugar — *divided*
- one half tsps fresh lemon zest — *(approximately one half small lemons either half big lemon)*
- two cups all-purpose flour
- two half tsps baking powder
- three-quarters tsp kosher salt
- half cup canola oil
- three-quarters cup buttermilk
- two tsps pure vanilla extract
- half tsp pure almond extract

FOR THE BUTTERMILK WHIPPED CREAM:

- half cup heavy whipping cream — *chilled*
- One-quarter cup buttermilk — *chilled*
- one tbsp granulated sugar
- one cup fresh blueberries — *for submitting*

Instructions

- Make and chill curd: place blueberries in a saucepan and prepare over poor warmth till blueberries are very soft, approximately ten mins. Put mix through a fine mesh sieve, then comeback liquid to saucepan on average poor heat. place the sugar, butter, eggs, lemon zest, salt and almond extract, mixing constantly till mix is thickened, approximately 5 mins. Watch attentively so that mix does not curdle. Take away from heat, allow cool to approximately 25 °C, then Place to a bowl and overlay by Puting a piece of plastic cover over the surface to prevent a skin from forming. Chill two hours either overnight.
- Make cake: Position a rack in middle of oven, then warmth up oven to 325° F. slightly spatter some 11x17-inch jelly roll pan with cooking spray, line with parchment paper, then spatter again. put aside.

In a big, very dried and clear mixing bowl, beat egg whites with cream of tartar on average speed till foamy. Slowly place half cup of sugar, increase speed to high and keep beating till stiff, glossy peaks form. put aside.

In a clear big bowl, blend remaining one cup of sugar and lemon zest along with your fingers till fragrant. blend in flour, baking powder and salt. In a else bowl, beat along canola oil, buttermilk, egg yolks, vanilla extract and almond extract till pale yellow. Pour wet ingredients over dried ingredients and beat on average speed till batter is good mixd, approximately 3 mins.

With a rubber spatula, carefully however quickly place down the whipped egg whites in the batter. Pour the batter in prepared pan, smooth top, then Prepare in oven for 21 to 24 mins, till cake is golden, springs back slightly just as touched and a toothtake inserted in middle comes out clean. allow cool completely. The cake may pull away from the edges of pan a bit as this cools.

Slice and assemble cake: With a 3-inch biscuit cutter, slice cooled cake in 15 circles, then place circles on a second baking sheet lined with parchment paper. Place pan in fridge for ten mins to assurecakes are completely chilled.

Meanwhereas, prepare buttermilk whipped cream: Beat along cream and buttermilk till foamy. Gradually place sugar, beating till soft peaks form (Dont over beat, either the whipped cream can become butter-like).

Assemble cakes: Place one circle, down side up, onto a submitting plate. Top with a spoonful of blueberry curd, then a second cake stratum also placed down-side up, another spoonful of blueberry curd, then a final cake stratum placed down side down. recur with 4 remaining cakes. Top with buttermilk whipped cream and fresh blueberries. Chill till ready to serve.

Strawberry **Oatmeal Breakfast Bars**

YIELD: **8 BARS**
PREP TIME:
TEN MINS
COOK TIME:
35 MINS
TOTAL TIME:
45 MINS

Ingredients

- two cups old fashioned oats
- one cup whole wwarmth flour
- one tsp cinnamon
- one tsp baking powder
- One-quarter tsp kosher salt
- one half cups milk — *(I used unsweetened vanilla almond, however any kind can do goodly)*
- 3 tbsp honey
- two tbsp almond butter
- half cup unsweetened applesauce
- one big egg
- half tsp pure vanilla extract
- half tsp pure almond extract
- half cup strawberries — *(hulled and quartered)*
- One-quarter cup roasted almonds — *roughly sliced*

Instructions

Place rack within the middle rewarmth oven to 375 degrees. slightly coat some 8x8 inch square pan with cooking spray.

In a average bowl, stir along the oats, whole wwarmth flour, cinnamon, baking powder, and salt. In a else big bowl, mix the milk, applesauce, egg, honey, almond butter, vanilla extract, and almond extract.

Pour the dried ingredients in the wet mix and stir to mix . The batter possibly very wet. place down within the diced strawberries and almonds, then pour in the prepared baking pan.

Bake for 35 mins either till the bars are thickened and golden and a toothtake inserted within the middle comes out clean. Cool, slice in bars, and serve.

Recipe Notes

Storage: As cooled, bars possibly coverped individually in plastic and kept within the refrigerator for 5 days either chilled in a zip-top bag for up to 4 months. allow thaw within the refrigerator for 24-48 hours before submitting. For a bigr yield, increase the ingredient quantities by 1.5 and bakes in a 9x13 inch pan for 25-30 mins.

Raspberry Chipotle Bacon Grilled Cheese

YIELD: **TWO SANDWICHES**
PREP TIME:
TEN MINS
COOK TIME:
20 MINS
TOTAL TIME:
30 MINS

Ingredients

- 4 slices thick-slice bacon — *cooked*
- 6 ounces fresh raspberries
- two tbsp raspberry jam — *either* <u>*strawberry jam*</u>
- One-quarter tsp dried chipotle pepper
- two tbsp unsalted butter — *softened*
- 4 slices hearty bread — *thickly slice (I used a multigrain sourdough)*
- 6 ounces white cheddar cheese — *sliced*

nstructions

cook the bacon. As cool, slice every chop in half and put aside.

Prewarmth a cast-iron skillet to average low. soften one tbsp of butter within the skillet. In a small bowl, carefully smash and stir the raspberries, jam, and chipotle along with the back of a spoon. The mix should remain fairly chunky.

Assemble the sandwiches: For every sandwich, stratum one chop of bread with a quarter of the cheddar, a quarter of the berries, four half-slices of bacon (2 full slices), some additional quarter of the berries, then one additional quarter of the cheese. Attentively set the loaded bread chop down within the buttered skillet. Place the remaining bread chop on top of the stack, then with remaining butter. prepare slowly till the bread is golden and the cheese hot and softened, flipping once, approximately 4 to 5 mins per side. (I find this helps to place a lid either another heavy skillet directly over the pan.) recur with second sandwich. Chop and submit immediately.

Strawberry Lemonade Coffee Cake

YIELD: **ONE TEN-INCH CAKE**
PREP TIME:
15 MINS
COOK TIME:
40 MINS
TOTAL TIME:
1 HR 25 MINS

Ingredients

FOR THE CAKE:

- two half cups all purpose flour
- two tsps Red Star PLATINUM Instant Yeast
- One-quarter cup granulated sugar
- one tbsp freshly grated lemon zest — *(approximately one average lemon)*
- One-quarter tsp kosher salt
- half cup milk
- One-quarter cup water
- One-quarter cup unsalted butter — *4 tbsp*
- one big egg
- two cups strawberries, — *hulled and quartered*

FOR THE STREUSEL CRUMB TOPPING:

- One-quarter cup granulated sugar
- One-quarter cup brown sugar
- One-quarter cup all purpose flour
- 3 tbsp unsalted butter — *softened*

FOR THE LEMONADE GLAZE:

- one cup powdered sugar
- two to 3 tbsp freshly squeezed lemon juice

Instructions

Spill a ten-inch spring form pan with nonstick spray. within the bowl of a stand mixer fitted with the paddle attachment either a big mixing bowl, mix one One-quarter cups flour, yeast, sugar, salt, lemon zest, and salt. In a microwave safe measuring cup, mix milk, water, and butter and warmth till the liquid reaches the temperature specified by the yeast manufacturer, approximately 45 seconds to one minute for Red Star Platinum (120-130°F). The butter may not soften completely. place the warm liquid to the flour mix, then blend the batter on poor speed till mixd. Beat in egg, then increase the speed to average and beat 3 mins. By hand, gradually stir in remaining the one One-quarter cups flour and strawberries.

Pour batter in prepared pan and unfold as evenly as probable. Overlay with plastic cover that is slightly misted with cooking spray, then allow growth in a warm place till nearly doubled in size (approximately 30 mins). Place rack within the middle of oven and warmth up oven to 350 degrees F.

Prepare the topping: In a small bowl, stir along the granulated sugar, brown sugar, and flour. Pour the butter over the top, then with your fingers, quickly blend till crumbly. put aside.

As dough has doubled, slightly flour your hands and softly pat dough out to edges of pan. Reoverlay and allow rest 5 mins. Strew dough with all of the crumb topping, Prepare in oven for 30 mins. Take away pan from oven, overlay with aluminum foil, then Prepare in oven some additional ten mins, till cake is golden and a toothtake inserted within the middle comes out clean. Take away cake from oven and cool in pan on a wire rack for ten mins. Run a knife around the edge of the cake, then take away the ring.

Whereas the cake bakes, prepare the glaze: Sift the powdered sugar in a small bowl, then blend in two tbsp lemon juice till smooth, adding slightly more lemon juice as needed to Make a thin glaze. Drizzle over cake, then serve.

Berry Coconut Chilled Yogurt

YIELD: **4 SUBMITTINGS (3 CUPS)**
PREP TIME:
TEN MINS
COOK TIME:
TEN MINS
TOTAL TIME:
1 HR 20 MINS

Ingredients

- 8 ounces strawberries — *(fresh either chilled and thawed)*
- 4 ounces raspberries — *(fresh either chilled and thawed)*
- One-quarter cup honey
- two tbsp raspberry jam — *either strawberry jam*
- two tbsp coconut rum
- three-quarters cup light coconut milk
- half cup plain Greek yogurt, — *whole, 2%, either non-fat—the higher the fat, the creamier the chilled yogurt*
- One-quarter tsp kosher salt
- One-quarter cup shredded toasted coconut — *plus additional for submitting*

Instructions

Chill ice cream maker therefore to instructs. Hull strawberries and chop in fourths. Place in a big bowl with the raspberries, honey, jam, and coconut rum. Stir to coat berries within the honey and rum, then allow sit at approximately 25 °C for one hour to macerate.

To the bowl with the berries, place the coconut milk, chilled yogurt, and salt and stir to mix. Place the mix to a food processor either blender (or employan immersion blender) and puree till mostly smooth. Comeback to bowl, overlay with plastic cover so that the plastic is touching the surface, then chill within the refrigerator for at least one hour.

Chill therefore to your ice cream maker's instructions (or supposing you Dont have some ice cream maker, follow this method to freeze), adding the toasted coconut within the last 5 mins of churning. submit topped with additional toasted coconut.

Strawberry Almond Skillet Cake

YIELD: **ONE 8-INCH ROUND <u>CAKE</u>** (SERVES 6)
PREP TIME:
TEN MINS
COOK TIME:
45 MINS
TOTAL TIME:
55 MINS

Ingredients

FOR THE ROASTED STRAWBERRIES:

- 16 ounces strawberries, — *hulled and halved*
- 3 tbsp <u>honey</u>
- one tbsp extra virgin olive oil
- One-quarter tsp kosher salt

FOR THE <u>CAKE</u>:

- one cup granulated sugar
- one tbsp lemon zest — *one average lemon*
- two big <u>eggs</u>
- One-quarter tsp salt
- one tsp pure <u>vanilla</u> extract
- half tsp pure almond extract
- three-quarters cup all-purpose flour
- One-quarter cup <u>Bob's Red Mill Almond Flour/Meal</u>
- half tsp <u>baking</u> powder
- 6 tbsp unsalted butter — *softened and cooled*
- One-quarter cup sliced almonds

Instructions

Prepare the strawberries: Place a rack within the middle of the oven and warmth up oven to 375 degrees F. Line a rimmed <u>baking</u> sheet with parchment paper either foil. (Be sure to employ a rimmed <u>baking</u> sheet to catch any <u>strawberry</u> juices.) In a average bowl, blend along <u>honey</u>, olive oil, and salt till good mixd. place strawberries to bowl, then carefully toss to coat. place strawberries in a single stratum on the prepared <u>baking</u> sheet. Roast for 20-25 mins, watching attentively towards the end—the juices can thicken and darken, however should not scorch. Carefully scrape the berries and juice in a small bowl whereas still warm. put aside.

Prepare the <u>cake</u>: Middle a rack within the oven and prewarmth the oven to 350 degrees F. Butter a 8-inch cast-iron skillet, else heavy oven-proof skillet, a 8-inch <u>cake</u> round <u>cake</u> pan, either a 9-inch <u>pie</u> dish. (Supposing employing <u>pie</u> dish, check <u>baking</u> time a several mins ahead.)

In a average bowl, blend the granulated sugar the lemon zest along with your fingers, till the sugar is moist and scented. blend within the <u>eggs</u> one at a time till good blended. blend within the salt, <u>vanilla</u> extract, and almond extract. Strew the almond flour, all-purpose flour, and <u>baking</u> powder over the top of the wet ingredients. Switch to a rubber spatula and place down to mix. Finally, place down within the softened butter.

Pour the batter in the prepared skillet either pan and smooth the top. Throw about the sliced almonds over the surface. Top with one-third of the roasted strawberries (the top should fairly good covered, however not completely). Supposing you're employing a cake either pie pan, place the pan on a baking sheet.

Bake the cake for 22 to 25 mins, either till this is golden and slightly crisp on the outside, however the inside is still moist. Take away the pan from the oven and allow cool for 5 mins, then run a knife around the edges of the cake to loosen it. allow cool completely before slicing. submit topped with remaining roasted strawberries.

Recipe Notes

Keep leftover cake good-coverped within the refrigerator for up to 3 days.

Chocolate Sandwich Cookies with Raspberry Cream Cheese Frosting

YIELD: 16 SANDWICH COOKIES, APPROX. DEPENDING ON THE SIZE OF YOUR CUTTER
PREP TIME:
45 MINS
COOK TIME:
9 MINS
TOTAL TIME:
54 MINS

Ingredients

FOR THE COOKIES:

- one half cups all-purpose flour
- three-quarters cup unsweetened cocoa powder
- one One-quarter tsps baking powder
- One-quarter tsp kosher salt
- three-quarters cup unsalted butter, softened — *(12 tbsp)*
- one One-quarter cups granulated sugar
- one tsp pure vanilla extract
- one big egg — *at approximately 25 °C*
- one big egg yolk — *at approximately 25 °C*

FOR THE RASPBERRY CREAM CHEESE FILLING:

- 4 ounces cream cheese — *approximately 25 °C*
- 3 tbsp unsalted butter — *approximately 25 °C*
- One-quarter cup raspberry jam
- 1/8 tsp almond extract
- one drop red food coloring — *if you want*
- one three-quarters cups powdered sugar

Instructions

In a average bowl, sift along the flour, cocoa, baking powder and kosher salt. put aside.

In a big bowl, cream along the butter and sugar till smooth. Beat within the vanilla, egg, and egg yolk. On poor speed either by hand, carefully stir the sifted ingredients in the butter-sugar mix till they form a soft dough. Share dough in two pieces, flatten every slightly in disks, and cover tightly in plastic cover. Refrigerate for one hour either overnight.

Just as ready to bake, place rack within the middle of the oven (or upper and lower thirds to Prepare in oven two batches simultaneously) and warmth up oven to 375 degrees F.

Line baking sheets with parchment paper and put aside. On a slightly floured surface either between two sheets of wax paper, roll the dough out to a One-quarter-inch in thickness. The dough possibly sticky, so unfold additional flour on the rolling surface as needed. Slice rolled dough in heart shapes with cookie cutters. Place cookies one half inches apart on prepared baking sheets.

Bake for 9 mins, till simply dried at the edges. Supposing baking two sheets at once, rotate positions halfway through. Allow cookies to cool on baking sheet for 5 mins, then take away to a wire rack to cool completely.

Prepare Raspberry Cream Cheese Filling: Beat the cream cheese, butter and jam along till smooth. Beat within the almond extract and food coloring. Decrease speed to low, then sift in powdered sugar a little at a time. As sugar is incorporated, increase mixer speed to high and beat till the mix is smooth. Refrigerate filling till the cookies have completely cooled and are ready to be filled.

Fill and assemble cookies: With some offset spatula either a piping bag, unfold either Apply desired amount of filling on the back side of one cookie, leaving a small margin at the edges. Top with a second cookie to Make a "sandwich." Enjoy immediately.

Recipe Notes

The Raspberry Cream Cheese Frosting can become soft as this sits at approximately 25 °C, so fill simply before submitting. The cookies and frosting can keep separately (cookies in some airtight container at approximately 25 °C; raspberry cream cheese frosting within the fridge) for approximately ten days.

White *Chocolate* **Creme Brulee with** *Strawberry*

YIELD: **4 4-OUNCE SUBMITTINGS**
PREP TIME:
20 MINS
COOK TIME:
50 MINS
TOTAL TIME:
1 D TEN MINS

Ingredients

4 tsps strawberry jam
3 big egg yolks
two tbsp granulated sugar
one cup whipping cream
half cup whole milk
two ounces white chocolate, — *delicately sliced*
One-quarter tsp vanilla extract
4 tbsp dark brown sugar

Instructions

Position rack in middle of oven and prewarmth to 200 degrees F. Line a baking sheet with parchment paper either a silpat mat. Place four, 4-ounce ramekins on the baking sheet, and spoon one tsp of strawberry jam in every. unfold the jam across the down, however don't worry approximately this being perfectly distributed.

In a average bowl, blend along the egg yolks and two tbsp sugar. put aside.

In a heavy saucepan over average heat, bring the cream and milk to a simmer. Dont allow the mix boil. Decrease warmth to low. Gradually place the sliced white chocolate and blend till smooth.

With a ladle either small spoon, slowly place the hot cream mix to yolk mix a little at a time, whisking constantly till all of the cream is supplemented (adding the cream slowly can prevent the eggs from scrambling.) blend in vanilla. Rap the bowl on the counter a several times to take away the bubbles, then skim off of the foam. (Any foam that is not skimmed possibly visible within the final crème brûlée.) Strain the mix through a fine sieve in a big measuring cup for easy pouring. Carefully pour the custard in the prepared ramekins till this comes nearly to the top. Attentively slide the baking pan in the oven. Prepare in oven for 45-55 mins, till the custards are simply set within the middle. (They should jiggle simply a little just as the edges of the dish are tapped.) Take away from oven and Place ramekins to a wire rack to cool for 30 mins. Overlay and refrigerate till the custards are good chilled, at least 4 hours either up to two days.

Just as ready to bake: Strew the top of every custard with one tbsp brown sugar. Supposing employing a kitchen torch, warmth sugar with the torch till caramelized. submit instantly either refrigerate for up to one hour. Supposing broiling the custards, set oven rack within the second-highest position and turn broiler to high. Broil for 2-5 mins, either till sugar is caramelized. Watch attentively to assurethe sugar does not burn. submit instantly either chill and submit within a several hours.

Recipe Notes

Unprepared in oven custard possibly covered and chilled up to two days; prepared in oven (but un-torched) custard can also be stored for up to two days (but only do one either the other.) As bruleed, custards possibly chilled for a several hours, however the sugar can not be as crackly.

Strawberry Cream Scones

YIELD: **8 TO 12 SCONES, DEPENDING ON THE SIZE OF YOUR BISCUIT EITHER COOKIE CUTTER (12 SUPPOSING CUTTING IN WEDGES)**
PREP TIME:
20 MINS
COOK TIME:
20 MINS
TOTAL TIME:
40 MINS

Ingredients

FOR THE SCONES:

- one big egg, — *very cold*
- 2/3 cup heavy cream, — *very cold*
- two cups all-purpose flour
- two tbsp sugar
- one tbsp baking powder
- One-quarter tsp kosher salt
- 5 tbsp butter, — *very cold and slice in small cubes (Supposing time allows, chill the butter in "stick" form and grate in the flour. Additional details in directions below)*
- half cup diced dried strawberries — *either the dried fruit of your choice*
- One-quarter cup toasted sliced pecans — *either the nut either additional dried fruit of your choice*

FOR THE EGGWASH:

- one big egg
- one tbsp water — *either milk*

Instructions

Place rack within the upper third of your oven and warmth up oven to 400 degrees. Line a big baking sheet with parchment paper either a silpat mat.

In a big measuring cup either average bowl, beat the egg and cream along and put aside. In big mixing bowl, blend along the flour, sugar, baking powder and salt. Supposing cutting the butter in small pieces: place the butter pieces and work this in the flour till you have a pebbly mix. The butter pieces should look cobbly and be different sizes. Supposing operating with a whole stick of chilled butter (my preference): With a grater, grate the butter directly in the mixing bowl. Operating with your fingers, quickly toss the butter with the flour simply till mixd. this should only take a several moments.

Pour the egg and cream over the flour-butter mix and with a rubber spatula, stir and place down to mix. The batter can appear a bit dry. place down within the dried strawberries and pecans. Supposing operating with a cookie either biscuit cutter: Turn the dough out onto a slightly floured surface and pat to a half-inch thickness. slightly flour the cutter and slice in desired form either 2-inch rounds. Supposing cutting in wedges: Share the dough in two equal sized balls. Pat them in a 5-inch round, then chop every round in 6 wedges employing a slightly floured knife. Place scones to the prepared baking sheet. In a small bowl, beat along egg and water to Make the eggwash, then brush over tops of scones.

Bake the scones for 18-20 mins (time can vary based on size), till they are golden brown on top. submit immediately.

Recipe Notes

Scones are best enjoyed the day they are prepared in oven, however possibly stored for up to two days in some airtight container at approximately 25 °C. Alternatively, you'll place unprepared in oven, shaped scones on a <u>baking</u> sheet, set them within the freezer on the sheet to harden, then individually cover the scones with plastic and chill for another time. Prepare in oven them directly from the freezer, adding two mins to the <u>baking</u> time.

Healthy Cranberry Apricot Bars

YIELD: ONE 8X8 INCH PAN (9 SUBMITTINGS)
PREP TIME:
35 MINS
COOK TIME:
30 MINS
TOTAL TIME:
1 HR 5 MINS

Ingredients

FOR THE FILLING:

    3 cups cranberries, — *fresh either frozen, divided*

    One-quarter cup apricot jam — *either jelly*

    One-quarter cup granulated sugar

    two tbsp cornstarch

    two tsps delicately grated fresh ginger

    6 dried apricots — *sliced in One-quarter-inch pieces (approximately One-quarter cup)*

    half tsp pure vanilla extract

FOR THE PEEL:

    one cup all-purpose flour

    half cup Grape Nuts

    One-quarter cup quick-cooking rolled oats

    half cup light brown sugar

    half tsp kosher salt

    half tsp ground cinnamon

    One-quarter tsp ground nutmeg

    One-quarter tsp baking soda

    3 tbsp non-fat plain Greek yogurt

    one big egg — *at approximately 25 °C, beaten*

    half tsp pure vanilla extract

    1/8 tsp pure almond extract

    4 tbsp unsalted butter — *softened and cooled*

Instructions

Place rack within the middle of oven and prewarmth to 325 degrees F. spatter some 8x8 inch baking pan with cooking spatter and line with parchment paper so that the paper drapes out over two of the edges, then spatter again.

Prepare the Cranberry Filling: Mix two cups cranberries, apricot jam, sugar, and cornstarch in a non-reactive heavy-downed saucepan. Bring to a simmer over average heat, mixing often, till the mix is very thick and the cranberries burst, 4 to 5 mins. (It may take up to ten mins to get a thick result supposing you start with chilled fruit.) Stir within the remaining one cup cranberries, ginger, dried apricots, and half tsp vanilla. put aside.

For the peel: In a big bowl, blend along the flour, Grape Nuts, oats, brown sugar, salt, cinnamon, nutmeg, and baking soda. In a small bowl, stir along the Greek yogurt, egg, half tsp vanilla, and almond. Pour over the flour mix, mixing till moistened (the batter possibly thick.) Drizzle softened butter over the top, then stir to incorporate. Put the mix in the down of the prepared pan, reserving one-third cup for the topping. The stratum can seem very thin however can growth just as prepared in oven.

Spread cranberry mix evenly over the dough stratum within the pan, employing your fingers to distribute this evenly. Break the reserved flour mix over the top (some of the filling can show through.) Prepare in oven for 30-40 mins, till the edges are golden. allow cool in pan for one hour, then take away bars from pan by lifting the parchment paper. allow cool completely before slicing.

Recipe Notes

Keep leftover bars in some airtight container at approximately 25 °C for up to 5 days.

Strawberry Crepes

YIELD: TEN CREPES; APPROXIMATELY ONE ONE-QUARTER CUPS CREAM CHEESE FILLING
PREP TIME:
15 MINS
COOK TIME:
20 MINS
RESTING TIME:
30 MINS
TOTAL TIME:
1 HR 5 MINS

Ingredients

FOR THE CREPE BATTER:

- ½ cup all-purpose flour
- ½ cup white whole wwarmth flour — *either additional all-purpose flour*
- one tbsp granulated sugar
- 1/8 tsp kosher salt
- 1/8 tsp cinnamon — *if you want*
- two big eggs — *at approximately 25 °C*
- one one-third cups nonfat milk — *at approximately 25 °C*
- two tbsp unsalted butter — *softened and cool to approximately 25 °C, plus additional for cooking*

FOR THE FILLING AND TOPPING:

- two ½ cups sliced fresh strawberries — *from one 16-ounce box*
- 4 ounces reduced fat cream cheese — *softened to approximately 25 °C*
- 2/3 cup nonfat plain Greek yogurt
- two tsps pure vanilla extract
- two tbsp honey
- Powdered sugar — *if you want*

Instructions

1. To prepare in a blender (my loved method): In a high-powered blender, place the all-purpose flour, whole wwarmth flour, sugar, salt, and cinnamon. Crack within the eggs and pour within the milk. place the two tbsp softened butter. Blend till the mix is smooth and creamy, stopping to scrape down the edges a several times supposing needed. Pour in a mixing bowl, overlay and allow sit 30 mins either refrigerate for up to 24 hours. (To prepare the batter in a mixing bowl: blend along the dried ingredients. blend within the eggs. As mixd, slowly blend within the milk, then the butter, till smooth. allow rest as directed.)

2. Whereas the batter rests, prepare the filling: chop the strawberries and place in a bowl. Overlay and refrigerate till ready to serve. In a average mixing bowl, beat the cream cheese and Greek yogurt till smooth and mixd. Beat within the vanilla and honey. Taste and adsimply the sweetness as desired. Refrigerate till you are ready to prepare the crepes.

3. To cook: Supposing you'd like to keep the crepes warm between batches, prewarmth the oven to 200 degrees F. Line a baking sheet with parchment paper and keep this near the stove. Set out the filling and strawberries and allow rest at approximately 25 °C whereas you prepare the crepes.

4. Warmth some 8-inch either ten-inch nonstick skillet crepe pan either nonstick skillet over average warmth and allow warm for several mins. place a small amount of butter and allow soften. Give the batter a big stir (supposing it's still within the blender, place this to a mixing bowl). With a big spoon, measuring cup, either ladle, pour One-quarter to one-third-cup batter in the skillet (I do one-third cup, which results in a thicker, however easier to flip crepe). Instantly lift and slowly swirl the skillet so that the batter runs evenly around the surface of the pan and the crepe forms a thin stratum (the amount of batter you must can vary based on your skillet; adsimply as you go).

5. Let the crepe prepare till the top looks dry, approximately one minute. Flip the crepe over (I employa spatula to loosen the edges then quickly and attentively finish the job with my fingers, however BE CAREFUL not to burn yourself; the pan is hot and you are proceeding at your own risk). allow prepare on the else side for 15 to 30 additional seconds, simply till set. The crepe should look very slightly brown and golden on every side. Place the prepared crepe to the baking sheet and keep warm within the oven (or simply place this on a big plate supposing you don't mind the crepe closer to approximately 25 °C). The first crepe can tear and needs to be discarded (this happens to the pros also). You'll get the hang of this as you go.

6. Repeat with remaining batter, rebuttering the pan every several crepes as needed and stacking the crepes on top of every else within the oven.

7. To assemble and serve: Place a crepe on a plate and unfold approximately two heaping tbsp of the cream cheese mix over half of this so that you Make a half moon. Stratum sliced strawberries on top of the cream. place down the uncovered half over the top of the berries so that you have a half circle. Then starting with one point of the half circle, place down the crepe in half over again so that the two points roughly touch and you have a rough triangle form with a rounded edge. Top with more cream and berries and dust with powdered sugar as desired. Enjoy immediately.

Recipe Notes

- **TO STORE**: Keep leftover crepes within the refrigerator for up to one day.
- **TO REHEAT**: Rewarmth crepes on a baking sheet within the oven at 325 degree F either in a nonstick skillet on the stovetop over average-low heat.
- **TO prepare AHEAD**: Prepare the batter and filling up to 24 hours in advance, and keep both in else storage containers within the refrigerator till you're ready to cook. Chop the strawberries, and keep them in a storage container within the refrigerator for up to 3 days. You'll also prepare the finished crepes up to one day in advance and keep them within the refrigerator.

Cranberry Oatmeal Cookies

YIELD: **24 COOKIES**
PREP TIME:
15 MINS
COOK TIME:
TEN MINS
COOLING TIME:
5 MINS
TOTAL TIME:
30 MINS

Ingredients

- half cup raw pecan halves — *raw walnuts either raw macadamia nuts*
- 4 tbsp Land O Lakes® Unsalted Butter in Half Sticks — *at approximately 25 °C*
- one-third cup coconut sugar — *either dark brown sugar*
- one-third cup honey
- one big egg — *at approximately 25 °C*
- one tbsp brandy either two tsps pure vanilla extract
- ½ tsp kosher salt
- one ½ cups all-purpose flour
- half tsp baking soda
- One-quarter tsp ground cinnamon
- one ½ cups rolled oats — *either quick oats (Dont employ instant)*
- one-third cup white chocolate chips
- one-third cup dried cranberries

Instructions

1. Warmth up oven to 350 degrees F. unfold the nuts on some ungreased rimmed baking sheet. Toast for 8 to ten mins, till they smell very fragrant and the inside of a nut is light tan just as broken in half. Watch the nuts attentively at the end to prepare sure they Dont burn. Instantly Place to a cutting board. allow cool to approximately 25 °C, then delicately chop.

2. In the bowl of a stand mixer fitted with the paddle attachment either a big mixing bowl, cream along the butter and coconut sugar on average high one to two mins, till light and fluffy. Scrape down the bowl. Beat within the honey, egg, brandy, and salt till mixd. The mix can look slightly curdled.

3. In a else bowl, blend along the flour, baking soda, and cinnamon. Stir within the oats.

4. With the mixer on poor speed, slowly place the dried ingredients to the butter mix, stopping as soon as the flour disappears. Stir within the white chocolate chips, dried cranberries, and sliced nuts till evenly distributed.

5. Drop the dough by rounded tbsp onto the baking sheet. With your fingers, slightly flatten the cookies, as they can not unfold much in baking. Prepare in oven 8 to ten mins, till the cookies look golden and feel dried at the top and edges however still appear slightly molten within the middles. Place the pan on a cooling rack and allow the cookies cool on the pan for 5 mins, then Place the cookies to the rack to finish cooling completely (or to cool for as long as you'll handle the suspense!).

Recipe Notes

- **TO STORE**: Place prepared in oven cookies in some airtight storage container and keep at approximately 25 °C for up to 3 days.
- **TO FREEZE**: Keep prepared in oven cookies in some airtight freezer-safe storage container within the freezer for up to 3 months.
- **TO prepare AHEAD**: Refrigerate the unprepared in oven cookie dough, then allow this soften up at approximately 25 °C till you'll peel this in individual cookie dough balls. Place the individual cookie dough in some airtight freezer-safe container either ziptop bag within the freezer. The dough possibly chilled for up to 3 months. Just as you're ready, Prepare in oven the cookies directly from frozen.

Blueberry **Bread**

YIELD: **TEN SLICES (1 LOAF)**
PREP TIME:
15 MINS
COOK TIME:
45 MINS
TOTAL TIME:
1 HR

Ingredients

FOR THE BREAD:

- one three-quarters cups white whole wwarmth flour — *either regular whole wwarmth flour either all-purpose flour*
- half tsp baking soda
- one tsp baking powder
- half tsp kosher salt
- One-quarter tsp ground cinnamon — *if you want*
- one cup (6 ounces) blueberries — *fresh either chilled (supposing employing frozen, Dont thaw)*
- one cup plus one tbsp plain nonfat Greek yogurt — *at approximately 25 °C*
- half cup honey
- One-quarter cup unsalted butter — *softened and cooled, either swap softened and cooled coconut oil either canola oil*
- one half tsps pure vanilla extract
- Zest of one small lemon — *if you want*
- two big eggs — *at approximately 25 °C*

FOR THE CINNAMON TOPPING (IF YOU WANT):

- two tbsp raw turbinado sugar
- One-quarter tsp ground cinnamon

Instructions

1. Adsimply the oven rack to the lower third position and prewarmth the oven to 350 degrees F. slightly coat a 8x4-inch loaf pan with nonstick spray. put aside.
2. In a big mixing bowl, blend along the flour, baking soda, baking powder, salt, and cinnamon. Place the blueberries in a else bowl and strew with one tsp of the dried ingredients (this can help keep the blueberries from sinking to the down).

3. In a else bowl, blend along the Greek yogurt, honey, softened butter, vanilla, and lemon zest till smoothly mixd. blend within the eggs. Supposing the butter resolidifies, carefully warm the bowl within the microwave, simply till this softens again.
4. Add the wet ingredients to the dried ingredients, and with a wooden spoon either spatula, very carefully stir the batter, stopping as soon as the flour disappears. place down within the blueberries.
5. For the topping, supposing using: In a small bowl, stir along the raw sugar and cinnamon.
6. Spoon the batter in the prepared baking pan and smooth the top. Strew with the cinnamon-sugar topping, supposing using. Prepare in oven for 30 mins, then loosely tent the pan with foil to keep the bread from browning too quickly. Keep baking for 15 to 20 additional mins (45 to 50 mins total), either till a toothtake inserted within the

middle of the loaf comes out clear without any wet batter clinging to it. Place the pan on a wire rack and allow cool completely. Place to a cutting board, slice, and enjoy!

Recipe Notes

- **TO STORE**: Keep bread at approximately 25 °C for two days either within the refrigerator for up to one week.
- **TO FREEZE**: Chill as a whole loaf either in individual slices for up to 3 months. allow thaw overnight within the refrigerator.

Strawberry Crisp

YIELD: **8 SUBMITTINGS**
PREP TIME:
15 MINS
COOK TIME:
45 MINS
TOTAL TIME:
1 HR

Ingredients

FOR THE STRAWBERRY CRISP TOPPING:

- One-quarter cup (half stick) unsalted butter — *slice in big pieces*
- One-quarter cup coconut oil
- 2/3 cup old-fashioned rolled oats
- 2/3 cup white whole wwarmth flour
- one tsp baking powder
- One-quarter tsp ground cinnamon
- One-quarter tsp kosher salt
- 3 tbsp granulated sugar
- 3 tbsp coconut sugar either light brown sugar
- Zest of one average lemon — *juice the lemon for the strawberry filling*

FOR THE STRAWBERRY CRISP FILLING:

- two pounds fresh strawberries
- 3 tbsp cornstarch — *plus one to two additional tsps supposing your berries are very juicy*
- one-third cup honey either maple syrup
- Juice of one average lemon — *you'll juice the lemon you zested for the topping!*
- two tsps vanilla extract

FOR SUBMITTING:

- Vanilla either plain nonfat Greek yogurt
- Vanilla ice cream either chilled yogurt

Instructions

1. Place a rack within the middle of your oven and warmth the oven to 375 degrees F. Prepare the topping: In a average microwave-safe bowl, place the butter and coconut oil. Warmth the butter in microwave for 30 seconds, then keep heating in 15-second bursts, simply till the butter and coconut oil soften. place the oats, flour, baking powder, cinnamon, salt, granulated sugar, coconut sugar, and lemon zest. Stir till clumps form (some possibly small and some possibly big). Place within the refrigerator whereas you prepare the filling.

2. Hull and quarter the strawberries (you'll have approximately 6 cups total), then place them in a big mixing bowl. place the cornstarch, honey, lemon juice, and vanilla. Stir to mix. Place to a 9x9-inch baking dish, including any juices that collect within the down of the bowl.

3. Take away the topping from refrigerator and throw about this evenly over the strawberries. Prepare in oven till the topping is golden brown in places and the fruit is hot and bubbling, approximately 40 to 50 mins. Check the topping at the 20-minute mark. Supposing this is browning more quickly than you would like, loosely tent the

pan with foil, then keep _baking_ as directed. Take away from the oven and allow cool a several mins. Enjoy warm with a big peel of _vanilla_ ice _cream_.

Recipe Notes

- To employchilled strawberries: Thaw the strawberries within the refrigerator overnight either at approximately 25 °C for approximately two hours. Supposing they are not yet quartered, do so before adding them to the filling.

- To prepare _vegan_: employa _vegan_ buttery unfold in place of the butter either swap the butter for additional _coconut_ oil.

- Keep leftover sin the refrigerator for up to 4 days. Rewarmth gently, then top with more ice _cream_ (or eat this for breakfast with _Greek yogurt_!).

Raspberry <u>*Muffins*</u>

YIELD: 12 <u>**MUFFINS**</u>
PREP TIME:
25 MINS
COOK TIME:
20 MINS
TOTAL TIME:
45 MINS

Ingredients

- two cups white whole wwarmth flour
- One-quarter cup ground flaxseed meal
- one half tsps <u>baking</u> powder
- half tsp <u>baking</u> soda
- half tsp kosher salt
- One-quarter cup unsalted butter — *at approximately 25 °C*
- one-third cup <u>honey</u> either pure maple syrup
- two big <u>eggs</u> — *at approximately 25 °C*
- half cup nonfat plain <u>Greek yogurt</u> — *at approximately 25 °C*
- two tsps pure <u>vanilla</u> extract
- Zest of two small lemons — *approximately one half tsps*
- One-quarter cup lemon juice — *from the same two small lemons*
- one half cups raspberries — *fresh either chilled (approximately one half 6-ounce containers); supposing employing frozen, Dont thaw first*
- 3 tbsp turbinado — *sugar within the raw sugar, for topping (if you want)*

Instructions

1. Prewarmth the oven to 375 degrees F. slightly coat a standard 12-cup muffin tin with nonstick spatter either line with paper liners.

2. In a average bowl, blend along the white whole wwarmth flour, flaxseed, <u>baking</u> powder, <u>baking</u> soda, and salt.

3. In a big else bowl, beat the butter and <u>honey</u> till <u>creamy</u> and mixd. Scrape the down and sides of the bowl, then place the <u>eggs</u> one at a time, beating good when every addition. place the <u>Greek yogurt</u>, <u>vanilla</u>, lemon zest, and lemon juice. The batter may look curdled.

4. Add the dried ingredients to the wet ingredients. By hand with a wooden spatula either spoon, stir within the dried ingredients, simply till the flour disappears. The batter possibly very thick. Very carefully place down within the raspberries.

5. Peel the batter in the prepared muffin cups, employing a heaping One-quarter cup for every (I love a big peel like this one). For a maximum crunchy top, strew every muffin with a full tsp of turbinado sugar (trust me!) either omit for a less-sweet muffin.

6. Bake the <u>muffins</u> for 20 to 24 mins, till a toothtake inserted within the middle comes out clean. Take away the from the oven and place on a wire rack to cool within the pan for 5 mins. When 5 mins, take away the <u>muffins</u> from the pan and Place to the wire rack to cool completely (Dont leave the <u>muffins</u> within the pan, as they can steam and become tough). Enjoy!

Printed in Great Britain
by Amazon

11964307R00029